CALIFORNIA SCENIC HIGHWAY No. 1

Including
Hearst Castle,
Monterey,
Carmel
and
Big Sur

1983 Published by Colourpicture Publishers, Inc.
76 Atherton St.
Boston, MA 02130

Distributed by James W. Cook
Cambria, California 93428

ISBN 0-938440-15-2

Text by Penelope P. Massey

PHOTO CREDITS:

Sandor Balatoni
Marian Blank
James Blank
William Bryan
Bob Glander

Overleaf: Sunset along the
Pacific Ocean

CONTENTS

CALIFORNIA SCENIC HIGHWAY No.1

"On no other coast that I know shall you enjoy, in calm, sunny weather, such a spectacle of ocean's greatness, such beauty of changing colour, or such degree of thunder in the sound."
Robert Louis Stevenson

California's first official scenic highway is Route 1 in Monterey County from the Carmel River south to the county border. This roadway and its scenic corridor have been preserved for the people of the Nation by action of the county and the State of California. It was dedicated September 21, 1966 at the Bixby bridge by Mrs. Lyndon B. Johnson.

Scenic Highway No. 1 is a famous stretch of rugged coastline between San Luis Obispo and Monterey, California. This highway is also known as the coast highway. Of all the roads which carry travelers over this land, none offers so much excitement per mile as this highway. Like an eagle, it soars then swoops along the very edge of the western coast on our North American Continent. It twists and winds within a stone's throw of the Pacific for some 300 of its 557-mile length, hemmed in by the ocean on one side and haze-covered mountains on the other. It presents bewhiskered sea otters, wintering grounds for thousands of monarch butterflies, an enchanted castle, gnarled wind-blown cypress trees, and captivating history.

From San Luis Obispo north, people can enjoy the abundance of seaside cliffs made mysterious by the fog which comes and goes at will. Morro Rock, in Morro Bay, is almost completely surrounded by the Pacific Ocean. It is the largest natural monolith of its kind along the California Coast. Morro Bay itself is a resort town with a lovely marina and waterfront. Also of great delight are the beaches at Cayucos and San Simeon, and the estuary and marshlands at Morro Bay State Park.

Hearst Castle at San Simeon, called La Cuesta Encantada, is an extravangance that must be seen. It is now a state historic monument and tours are conducted through the castle on a daily basis.

From San Simeon north to Carmel, the area is flanked on one side by the Santa Lucia Mountain Range and on the other by the rocky Pacific Coast. The visitor travels this breathtaking highway slowly, making frequent stops at scenic overlooks to take in the sea and the cliffs. No sense to rush this enjoyable part of the world. The natural beauty and tranquility are unparalleled whether you hike through redwood forests, picnic, camp, fish, or enjoy the beaches.

This region is known as a place to mediate and catch up with yourself. A beautiful part of the California coast in which to enjoy the beauties of nature.

Left: California Scenic Highway No. 1

From SAN LUIS OBISPO

to SAN SIMEON BEACH

San Luis Obispo is situated on San Luis Obispo Creek at the base of the Santa Lucia Mountains, about 12 miles from the Pacific Ocean and 107 miles northwest of Santa Barbara. It was founded in 1772 by Father Junipero Serra in the course of establishing his fifth mission. Seeing a resemblance to a bishop's mitre in two nearby volcanic peaks, he decided to name it Mission San Luis Obispo de Tolosa, or St. Louis, Bishop of Toulouse. Previous missions had been built with thatched roofs, and after burning several times, a tile-making technique was developed, making this one of the first churches to use such a roof.

San Luis Obispo is the county seat and center of a huge grain, livestock, poultry and dairy region. It also depends on tourism, commerce and its university population from California State Polytechnic College and Cuesta College.

Far left: Mission San Luis Obispo, was established in 1772, and the city grew up around this church. Now an historical museum, and a parish church. It was one of the first churches to be built with a tile roof.

Left: With the gentle backdrop of the Santa Lucia Mountains, San Luis Obispo is the county seat and center of a huge grain, livestock, poultry and dairy region.

Below: The Southern Pacific Sunset Limited train rounding famous hairpin curve near Poly College.

Overleaf: Aerial view of Morro Rock, Gibraltar of the Pacific.

Left: Harbor at Morro Bay.

Below: San Simeon Beach and Cove Area, located on Route 1 near Hearst San Simeon State Historical Monument. San Simeon is located between Monterey and San Luis Obispo, California.

Top and bottom right: Cayucos- cattle ranching area and summer vacation homes; great fishing from surf and pier and much from off shore boats; a great coastal attraction for the people of the San Joaquin Valley, which is an easy auto trip for a change of scenery; fine camping available in the area.

HISTORY OF THE HEARST CASTLE

William Randolph Hearst named it La Cuesta Encantada, the Enchanted Hill. Set against the verdant Santa Lucia Mountains on a coastal knoll, its 123 acres of gardens, terraces, pools and palatial guest-houses create a perfect setting for the magnificent Hispano-Moorish mansion, La Casa Grande.

The story of Hearst Castle is a long and colorful one. For the turrets, towers and temples that today crown this California hilltop did not spring into being overnight. The beginnings of today's world-celebrated "Enchanted Hill" started in 1865. In that year 43-year-old George Hearst, having made a fortune in investments in the mines of Nevada's Comstock Lode, and elsewhere, bought a 40,000-acre ranch for seventy cents an acre that lay adjacent to San Simeon Bay in northern San Luis Obispo Country. This was the first unit of what eventually became the huge San Simeon property…a 240,000 acre area of mountains, foothills, and valleys with an ocean front of more than fifty miles.

The son of a Missouri farmer, George Hearst became one of the richest mining tycoons of the West during the 19th Century. A loving, kind, and courteous man who loved work and politics, George Hearst was particularly known for his extreme generosity with money. He was very expedient in business matters and an excellent judge of mines, commanding up to $50,000 for a single consultation. Ultimately, he became a United States Senator. His wife, Phoebe Apperson Hearst, had an avid interest in philanthropy and art and was a woman of great culture and excellent tastes. Together they had one son, William Randolph, whom they called "Sonny". He was born in San Francisco on April 29th, 1863.

Little William loved his father dearly, though he spent little time with him since his father was frequently away for long periods on business. William did, however, spend his young life with his mother, and she in turn guided and supervised his upbringing under great care. William grew to love culture and art with the same fervour as his mother. He also inherited his father's humor, generosity with money, and love of the outdoors. The three of them frequently used the 40,000-acre ranch, called "Camp Hill", for picnicking and camping. By the time William reached his teens, he liked nothing better than to share the informal life on the ranch.

When William's father died in 1891, his mother succeeded to ownership of the ranch, and it wasn't until her death in 1919 that the title to the property passed to William. When William married and began his own family, he continued to use Camp Hill as a camping place with his children, though the sojourns began to take on a regal elaborateness which was later to became the trademark of his grandiose entertaining style. Huge circus tents were set up as temporary "guest houses" for his groups of friends, and the San Simeon hilltop parties began in earnest. Other tents were pitched for all the chauffeurs, nurses, servants and tutors. What a scene it must have been! At this time began the transformation of the San Simeon hilltop from a summer vacation spot to the huge rambling Hearst Castle that presently occupies the site. Work on the first unit of the group of buildings began in the fall of 1919 and continued with hardly an interruption until William's death more than three decades later.

Left: View of La Casa Grande from the gardens. The twin towers house 36 carillon bells from Belgium and ornate bedrooms in the Celestial Suite.

Left: The Neptune Pool sparkles in sunlight atop the Enchanted Hill. 104ft. long and graduating from 3½ ft. to 9½ ft. in depth, the pool contains 345,000 gallons of mountain spring water.

Overleaf: Within the 123 acres at the crest of the Enchanted Hill nestle magnificent gardens, pools, statues, walks, and fountains.

Above: Completed in 1921, Casa Del Sol was named for a view of the setting sun, and contains 18 guest rooms on 3 levels. A bronze copy of Donatello's DAVID tops the 17th Century Venetian fountain.

Left: A bed of deciduous Azalea with the Ares Ludovisi in the background. The Greek God of War is portrayed, resting with the God of Love, Eros, copied from an original by Petrilli.

Below: Sekhmet, the Egyptian Goddess of War, is one of the oldest objects at Hearst Castle. It dates to the 18th Dynasty, some 3500 years ago. These lion-headed statues are carved in diorite, a durable igneous stone.

By 1919, William Randolph Hearst was well launched on his career as newspaper owner and publisher of the San Francisco EXAMINER, a paper which had been owned by his father. He had money to spend, and a dream of owning and building a spectacular residence, on a commanding hill overlooking the Pacific Ocean. In the planning of his hilltop showplace, the first requirement...that of providing adequate quarters for groups of guests...was well taken care of, first in three "cottages" and later in the Castle itself. In 1919, 1920, and 1921 the guesthouses...La Casa del Mar, "The House of the Sea"; La Casa del Monte, "The House of the Mountain"; and La Casa del Sol, "The House of the Sun"...were completely built. Four years later, "La Casa Grande", the main castle became W.R. Hearst's living quarters, though it was not finished. It really never was finished; and in fact, never would be since Hearst was a compulsive builder and could never stop adding on. The San Simeon hilltop was renamed La Cuesta Encantada, "The Enchanted Hill"...and indeed, that IS what it became.

Hearst hired one of the first women to practice architecture for this awesome venture. Julia Morgan was her name, and she possessed not only tremendous ability as an architect, but was in perfect harmony with the grandiose dreams Hearst had in mind. The two of them became "architects in fellowship" and provided each other with the perfect blend of critical eye, technical experience, and building knowledge. Where one had a weakness, the other had strength. And thus began the paradise on the Enchanted Hill.

The three "cottages", as he called them, were truly handsome and spacious structures each containing from ten to eighteen rooms, with white walls and red-tiled roofs, and are excellent examples of the Spanish Renaissance style of architecture. The names given each was suggested by the view to be had from its windows; thus, La Casa del Mar faces the broad expanse of the Pacific, La Casa del Monte looks over the successive ridges of the Santa Lucia Mountains, and La Casa del Sol fronts westward toward the setting sun.

After the cottages, plans for La Casa Grande were drawn and redrawn to meet all the criteria required by Hearst. It had to have something of the informality that had prevailed on the hill in earlier days, and it had to provide an appropriate setting for Hearst's ever-growing collections of antique furniture and objects d'art. Ultimately, it was constructed from several European castles, and untold millions of dollars. All told, it has thirty-eight bedrooms, thirty-one bathrooms, fourteen sitting rooms, a kitchen, two libraries, a movie theater, a billiard room, an Assembly Hall, a Refectory (or dining hall), a beautiful indoor Roman swimming pool, and an exquisite 104-foot outdoor Neptune Pool.

The facade has a distinctive Mediterranean look, (mostly Spanish), and the decor is primarily medieval or Renaissance. As previously mentioned, Hearst was an ardent and tireless art collector, and during his entire adult life managed to assemble the largest, most valuable collection ever held by a private individual. Priceless 16th-century Dante chairs, 18th-century Sheffield platters, Kermanshah carpets, teakwood floors, Persian rugs, marble floors, French-Renaissance fireplaces from the 16th-century, magnificent tapestries, Hispano-Moresque ceilings, Grecian urns, Roman statues, and countless other objects d'art held a special place in each room.

While La Casa Grande was being constructed, the grounds were being developed on a scale no less magnificent. The outstanding feature is the outdoor Neptune Pool, enlarged twice by Hearst before he was finally satisfied with its size. It holds a mere 345,000 gallons of spring water! It is a creation that has been pronounced perfect in all respects, from its marble floor and graceful colonnades to the lovely Greco-Roman temple that stands at one side. From the pool, marble stairways lead to a succession

Overleaf: Refectory, in La Casa Grande, is the great dining hall that saw famous personalities seated at 300-year old monastery tables. Silk banners are from Siena, Italy.

Gilt Spanish columns frame the entrance to The Assembly Room at Hearst Castle. 16th Century choir stalls from Italian Monasteries panel the lower walls.

Pool and billiard tables rest on travertine floors in The Game Room of La Casa Grande. A rare Gothic tapestry and antique Persian tiles add color. Scenes of bullfights adorn the antique Spanish ceiling.

The Assembly Room in La Casa Grande is 86 ft. long, 32 ft. wide and some 24 ft. high. Renaissance tapestries hang above 400-year-old walnut choir stalls from Italian monasteries.

The Main Library in La Casa Grande contains one of the world's best collections of Greek Pottery. These date from the 2nd Century B.C. to the 8th Century BC. Rare books are housed in elaborate cabinets.

Left: The Cardinal Richelieu Bed is located in Casa Del Monte, built in 1920. Carved in planks of black walnut, it dates to the 17th Century and represents one of the finest carvings at Hearst Castle.

Below: The Della Robbia Room, located in La Casa Grande, displays fine examples of glazed terra cotta work from the workshops of the Della Robbia family in Florence, Italy.

of formal gardens where a profusion of flowers and blossoming shrubs border the walks and twine about ancient urns, satyrs, sundials, and other garden ornaments. Winding gracefully about the crest of nearby Orchard Hill is a vine-covered pergola more than a mile in length, under which guests were accustomed to stroll while enjoying the panoramic view of mountains and sea at every turn.

All the landscaping was overseen by a horticultural expert from England named Nigel Keep, and a permanent staff of twenty gardeners. Nigel Keep came to work for Hearst in 1919 and spent his entire life working at San Simeon. Working under torchlight, all the gardening was done at night, reportedly because Hearst could not bear the sight of a wilting blossom. He also could not bear to see a tree cut down. Once while on route from San Francisco, Hearst stopped at Paso Robles and while there, learned that some thirty tall cypress trees were about to be cut down. He promptly bought the entire lot, had each encased in a wooden box, carefully watered and fertilized for a period of two years, then transferred to San Simeon. Today they stand in graceful rows adjacent to the outdoor swimming pool.

Hearst not only loved art and nature, he also had a tremendous interest in animals, and he set about collecting them with the same enthusiasm and grandiose scale as other things. Having decided that San Simeon must have a zoo, he created the world's largest privately owned aggregation of wild animals. He put aside some 2,000 acres of hillside and canyon in which the animals could roam, and enclosed the area with ten miles of eight-foot-high wire fence. Into this compound were turned close to a hundred species of domestic and jungle beasts.

His first animal acquisition was a herd of pure white fallow deer from Asia. To that he added black buffaloes from Montana, musk oxen from Greenland, emus from Australia, camels, elk, antelope, kangaroos, zebras, llamas, ostriches, bears, monkeys, lions, tigers, and many other species from all over the world. When weekend guests arrived, their favorite diversion was a visit, at feeding time, to the quarters of the caged birds and animals located a little distance down the hill from the Castle.

Although the compounds and cages and pits where the animals once lived have long stood empty, one striking reminder of that earlier period is to be seen at the San Simeon of today. When, in the late 1930's, the zoo was abandoned and the animals were presented to various West Coast cities, several kinds of beasts remained behind. Among these were the zebras, which adapted themselves so well to their environment that several wandered off into the back-country. There they throve and multiplied, and today they number several scores. It is by no means unusual for present-day visitors, on their way to or from the Castle, to catch sight of groups of the picturesque creatures peacefully grazing on the hillsides, together with tahrs, elk, and aoudads.

There is another part to the story of the Enchanted Hill, besides its magnificence in structure and decor. The golden days of extravagant entertainment is certainly a chapter in William Randolph Hearsts' life worth mentioning.

Many tales grew about the famous weekends at San Simeon. People constantly talked about the wild parties and scenes there; but in truth, the parties were not nearly as "wild" as people imagined. William Hearst was basically a quiet man, almost retiring in his ways. The hours at San Simeon were very informal and the dress was always casual. He conducted his vast business empire with an air of informality rarely seen within most corporations. His temperament was mercurial...not explosive in nature...but sometimes he was given to childish pouting when things didn't please him.

The entertainment he is probably most remembered for are the many picnics held on the ranch. Often he would go horsebackriding for three or four days, feeding his guests extravagantly during outdoor "picnics" within the confines of his 40,000 acre ranch.

Above: Portrait of William Randolph Hearst hangs at the far end of the Gothic Study in La Casa Grande. It was from here that Mr. Hearst directed his vast business empire. Rare books are housed in the ornate shelves.

Overleaf: Interior of the Roman Pool gleams with hand-set mosaic tiles. Alabaster lamps give a moonlight effect and sparkle on tiles of 18 carat gold, fused in glass.

At the Castle, the casualness was also apparent. The only hour promptly attended by everyone was at 7:30 p.m. in the magnificent Assembly Hall. Here he greeted his guests punctually and at 9:00 p.m. dinner was served in the Refectory. Unless, of course, there was some interesting entertainment taking place in the Assembly Hall, in which case Hearst would delay the dinner hour. After dinner, everyone would go off to see pre-released Hollywood features in his 50-seat theater. Hearst was enthralled with the cinema, and began looking into the possibilities of making motion pictures. He was an avid photographer and enjoyed the challenge of creating his own home movies by casting his famous guests as the stars. Ultimately, he made history as the founder of the first newsreel called the Hearst-Selig Weekly which covered Woodrow Wilson's first inauguration. THE PERILS OF PAULINE in which Pearl White starred, was another major achievement by Hearst, and has gone down in history as the first movie serial ever produced.

Later, Hearst got together with M-G-M and moved his production facilities to California. He produced the first musical in sound called BROADWAY MELODY, and other pictures such as GOING HOLLYWOOD, THE BIG HOUSE, PEG O' MY HEART, and WHITE SHADOWS IN THE SOUTH SEAS. Hearst also recognized young talent, and was responsible for launching the careers of such greats as W.C. Fields, Dick Powell and Marion Davies.

Unfortunately, the depression of the thirties arrived, striking everyone's pocket book, including Hearsts'. He reportedly lost some $7,000,000 trying to keep his movie productions alive, and finally came to realize that this venture was too expensive even for him to continue. His love of movie production was replaced with radio broadcasting, and he used that medium, in conjuction with his newspapers to influence public opinion on major political issues.

Hearst built a "mini-San Simeon" closer to Hollywood with the same zest and planning as the main Castle. It was even more informal in atmosphere, and it quickly became a gathering place for the movie set. Hearst did not enjoy this place as much as San Simeon, particularly because it was considered finished architecturally, and he couldn't keep "adding-on" as he continued to do at San Simeon. He substituted his deep seated desire to build with creating and giving masterful parties for which he will always be remembered.

His favorite parties were costume parties. He invented every kind of costume party theme imaginable, which in turn eliminated all formality at his gala affairs. Imagine Clark Gable decked out in shorts and knee socks as a Boy Scout, and Joan Crawford and Norma Shearer dressed as "frilly little Shirley Temples"! Indeed, it happened at one of the first of Hearsts' extravaganzas called "a kid's party". Another memorable occasion revolved around an early American theme, with Hearst dressed as James Madison, his five sons as young sailors, Norma Shearer as Marie Antoinette, and a five-tiered cake designed after Independence Hall.

His last public hoopla was in 1938 when he celebrated his seventy-fifth birthday and invited over three-hundred people. The theme was a three-ringed circus, and he was the ringmaster. Everyone was there...Jack Warner, Carole Lombard, Bette Davis, Henry Fonda, James Stewart, Loretta Young, David Niven, Mary Astor, and on...riding merry-go-rounds under huge circus tents in every circus costume imaginable until the wee hours of the morning.

At the age of eighty-eight, William Randolph Hearst died. He left a legacy of over $400,000,000 and a philosophy of charming simplicity: "Pleasure is worth what you can afford to pay for it". He died, the King of Entertainment.

Hearst Castle at San Simeon is now a State Historic Monument. The public finally has a firsthand chance to walk through this palacial residence and museum, and to relive an era of private entertaining which most likely will never be duplicated.

Left: Picturesque statuary is seen at many points on the Enchanted Hill. These expensive imports helped William Randolph Hearst spend $40,000,000 in pre-inflation money developing the "Ranch" he loved. This is one of the three guest cottages.

Below: View of the fabulous Hearst Castle which contains 100 rooms filled with rare works of art. 3 guest houses are located in the garden and contain another 46 rooms of art treasure.

Right: Hearst Castle at night.

BIG SUR
A MASTERPIECE
OF MOUNTAIN, SEA,
AND SKY

"...go where you will
you have but to pause
and listen to hear the voice
of the Pacific."

Robert Louis Stevenson

"On no other coast that I know shall you enjoy, in calm, sunny weather, such a spectacle of Ocean's greatness, such beauty of changing colour, or such degrees of thunder in the sound."

"These long beaches are enticing to the idle man. It would be hard to find a walk more solitary and at the same time more exciting to the mind."

Robert Louis Stevenson

''The waves come in slowly, vast and green, curve
their translucent necks, and burst with a surprising
uproar, that runs, waxing and waning, up and down
the long key-board of the beach. The foam of these
great ruins mounts in an instant to the ridge of the
sand glacis, swiftly fleets back again, and is met and
buried by the next breaker.''

''At sunset, for months together, vast, wet,
melancholy fogs arise and come shoreward from
the ocean.''

Robert Louis Stevenson

BLOOD FOR RUBLES – THE PERILS OF THE CALIFORNIA SEA OTTER

"The mothers followed me at a distance, like dogs,
calling to their young with a voice like the wailing
of an infant; and when the young ones heard their
mother's voice, they wailed too. I sat down in the
snow, and the mothers came close up and stood ready
to take the young ones from my hand if I should set
them down.... After eight days I returned to the same
place and found one of the females at the spot where
I had taken the young, bowed down with deepest sorrow.
Thus she lay, and I approached without any sign of
flight on her part. Her skin hung loose, and she
had grown so thin in that one week that there was
nothing left but skin and bones."
From the Journal of Dr. Georg Wilhelm Steller 1741

This unique and wonderful mammal cavorts among kelp beds like an underwater quarterback, uses tools to crack open sea urchin and abalone, never abandons her young, has such exquisite fur that men once killed each other to get it, caused the discovery of the northeast American coast by the rest of the world, was pushed to near extinction, and has staged a dramatic comeback.

This "clown of the kelp beds" has an amazing history, an endearing life style, and complex relationship with nature and man.

It was European explorers who first saw the "great river of fur" in 1741, when Vitus Bering sailed into the sea which now bears his name. Sea otters at that time ranged from Baja California to Alaska, and along the North Pacific rim to northern Japan. These early explorers, members of a Russian expedition, didn't know what those bundles of swimming fur were. The called them bears, beavers, and even apes; but no matter what they were, they would ultimately save the lives of explorers.

Bering set out on his expedition to discover land on the other side of Siberia, land they knew existed but had never seen. He sailed east from the Kamchatka Peninsula in a very poorly built ship called the St. Peter. It wasn't long before the ship began to fall apart, and his crew became ill from malnutrition. In a storm, the St. Peter was shipwrecked on a group of islands, later to be named Commander Islands. Bering died of scurvy, as did much of his crew, but those who survived took shelter in fox dens, often being attacked by the brazen artic blue foxes themselves.

There wasn't much on these barren unfriendly islands, except sea cows which occasionally would swim close to shore and could be slaughtered for food, and sea otters which were not a gourmets delight but certainly had wonderful fur for warm clothing and blankets. Once the crew began to regain strength, they took sections of the shipwrecked St. Peter and rebuilt a new, smaller ship, also called the St. Peter. After nine months of desolate and lonely living, they set sail, returning to Kamchatka Peninsula with a boat load of sea otter pelts. The new St. Peter leaked as badly as the first, and most of the cargo, including the sea otter pelts was thrown overboard to help keep the ship afloat. At least one sailor disobeyed orders and hid a few pelts under his bunk. Although not in good condition, the pelts made it to land in 1742.

The Bering expedition was considered a failure in every way except one. The sea otter pelts sparked a considerable amount of interest among traders, particularly in China. Wealthy Chinese were known to wear luxurious fur coats and Chinese merchants found a ready market for sea otter pelts. The pelts command very high prices, often hundreds of dollars if they were of high quality. The high price, combined with the abundance of sea otters, brought a stampede of Russian hunters.

Two factors worked against the otter. One, a most unusual characteristic, is the fact that the fur is prime at all times of the year. They never get shaggy from shedding, since their pelage grows and falls out much the way a human's hair does. This year-round primeness was one of the most critical factors which led to their near extinction, since they could be commercially hunted all twelve months of the year. The other factor which worked to the otter's disadvantage is the fact that they are monogamous and not prolific. They welp only one pup at a time, and the pup stays with its mother for an unusually long period of time. Since pups are born any time, they could be caught every month of the year with ease.

The Russians began building boats which they called SHITIKAS, meaning "stitched together". And stitched together they were! The Russians were hunters, not sailors, and knew nothing about building techniques and materials for their hunting boats. Rough cut boards were tied together with pelts to form a hull and reindeer skins were used as sails. Most of the SHITIKAS were not fit to float, let alone sail, but somehow a few managed to make it as far as Commander Islands. The otters found by Bering and his crew were still there and they slaughtered some 1,600 of them. In today's market, those pelts would bring as much as $90,000.

Most of the SHITIKAS were lost at sea, and many Russians also lost their lives at the hands of the island natives, whom they called Aleuts. The name was derived from the phrase ALIK UAIA which the Russians often heard from the natives. It tranlates into "what is it?", a question the islanders always asked when the Russians arrived in their stitched-together boats.

The Aleuts were the most skillful of all sea otter hunters. The method, a SPEARING SURROUND, was considered orthodox and had been used years by their ancestors. It involved the use of dozens, and sometimes a hundred or more kayaks, spread out in a wide circle and surrounding the sea otters. It was well known that these mammals must surface for air, usually at minute intervals, and can stay under water for no more than four minutes. When the otter came to the surface, everyone shouted to make the animal dive again, giving it little time to fill its lungs with air. This process was repeated until the otter's dives became increasingly shorter. Finally exhausted, the otter would come to the surface, and the Aleuts would spear it.

The Russians learned to use the SPEARING SURROUND, and the killings continued. In 1757 a Russian cargo of 3027 sea otter pelts fetched 187,268 rubles, or nearly $150,000. News of all this potential wealth spread, and hunters from Europe, Asia, and North America traveled up and down the northeastern continent seeking their fortunes. Discoveries of the sea otter herds helped set the boundaries of todays world, but the shy bewhiskered otter was nearly exterminated in the process.

Finally in 1911, the United States, Russia, Japan, and Great Britian agreed to stop killing the sea otters. Even before federal protection began, the California sea otter was believed by many to be extinct. In 1938 however, a California resident spotted a herd of nearly a hundred in Monterey County along the Big Sur coast. It was the only remaining colony south of Alaska. The otters of British Columbia, Washington, Oregon, and Baja California were gone.

Today, the Big Sur herd numbers perhaps 1,000. Over the past few years, surplus Amchitka otters have been transported by wildlife biologists to their former Alaska and Northwest habitats in hopes of increasing their population. In certain areas, otters have begun to outgrow their food supply and either must be harvested or airlifted to other suitable locations.

The California sea otter is four to five feet long and weighs 70 to 80 pounds when mature. Though it looks more like a land animal, with ears, legs, whiskers, and thick fur, it rarely comes on land but prefers instead to spend its life among kelps beds. It is considerably friendlier than many other mammals and has been known to beg a squid or sea urchin dinner from divers so long as it isn't touched.

Sea otters have a unique waterproofing blanket of air in their lush fur which allows them to float. They spend much of their waking hours grooming themselves with such fastideousness that often a visitor looks upon this behaviour as out and out vanity. In truth, if any amount of debris were to penetrate the fur, the otter would simly sink. It also as a thermal barrier against the cold since it doesn't have layers of fat or blubber to keep it warm.

The sea otter has an unusual ability to use tools for smashing open shellfish and other crustacians. This phenomena puts the sea otter among a very select few who habitually use tools. Only man, chimpanzees, an Egyptian vulture, and the Galapagos woodpecker finch are known to use them. Sea otters will dive to the bottom of kelp beds, sometimes as deep as a hundred feet, gather up an armful of sea urchings, mussels or abalone, and a rock. Returning to the surface, it rolls on its back, places the rock atop its furry stomach and while holding a mussel with its front feet, repeatedly whacks it against the rock until it breaks open. Sometimes it requires ten or so whacks, other times as many as forty or more, depending on the type of shellfish being opened. Every thirty seconds or so, the sea otter wraps its arms around the booty and rolls over in the water to clean off any food scraps and debris on its chest.

They have the ravenous appetite of a teenager, eating 15 to 20 pounds or one-fourth of its body weight, a day. For this reason abalone fishermen along the Big Sur coast want the otters removed from commercial abalone beds, a controversy which has been going on since the 1960's. Staunch supporters of the sea otter continue to rally, stating that these animals need a refuge. Also, they report that abalone is becoming scarce in areas where there is no otter population. Therefore, the otter shouldn't take the entire blame.

Aside from the abalone fishermen wanting population management, sea otters are facing other perils. Along Big Sur, the most common danger is boat propellers. Silt is another danger since it floats to the ocean floor and kills marine plants. With plants gone, the shellfish disappear, and there goes the otters food supply. Oil slicks and other pollutants can devastate an entire herd in no time. These dangers, of course, present a threat to all wildlife near the waters edge.

Of greatest concern is the effect on nature's ecosystem should the sea otters disappear. An otter's community is the kelp bed. It supports and shelters all kinds of marine life of importance to the otter. Kelp is a strange form of seaweed which grows as much as a foot or two a day, making it the fastest growing plant in the world. It has been harvested for many years by man as a food supplement, fertilizer, and a chemical and mineral source. An important substance found in kelp is algin, which is used primarily as a stabilizer or emulsifier in such things as ice cream, cake icing, salad dressing, paints, dyes, glues, and many other products. The greatest danger to a kelp bed are sea urchins which feed on kelp beds. And....the best sea urchin killer is the sea otter. Thus the sea otter depends on the kelp bed as much as the kelp bed depends on the otter, an ecological cycle which should be maintained intact.

Indeed the sea otter has suffered many problems. Research, amid controversy, amid just plain love of these mammals will certainly continue. No matter what the problems, one thing is certain. The future is promising, and visitors will continue to don binoculars along Big Sur, hoping to catch a glimpse of this marvelous clown of the kelp.

CARMEL

Carmel, a center for artists and writers since the turn of the century, sits on a curving beach at the foot of rolling hills...one of the loveliest spots along the California coast. The architecture found here is a mixture of every whim and style of the literary and artistic populace, and its individualism is fiercely protected.

Settled during the early 1600's, it was chartered as a village in 1916 and is governed by a mayor and council. In 1770, Father Junipero Serra founded the Mission San Carlos Borromeo here, one of the oldest missions in California. The remains of Father Serra rest at the foot of its high altar. Carmel has no cemetery, no jail, and no industry except handicrafts which attracts a lively tourist trade.

Left top: Carmel Plaza, one of the many beautiful shopping areas in Carmel which contain shops that display their wares from all over the world.

Left bottom: Mission San Carlos Borromeo, established in June 1770, is one of the oldest missions in California.

Right: This scene shows the gentle fog rolling toward Carmel Bay with its crescent-shaped white sandy beach. The seaside town of Carmel-by-the-Sea is nestled among the pine and cypress trees.

49

Top left: It was at the Bixby bridge that Mrs. Lyndon B. Johnson dedicated California's first official scenic highway—Route 1—on September 21, 1966.

Left: At the end of a beautiful day at Carmel Beach, many varied footprints can be seen reflecting the day's activities of sun bathing.

Above: Point Lobos State Reserve, derives its name from its colonies of California and Steller's sea lions. The sound of their hoarse barking is carried inland from the offshore rocks at Punta de los Lobos Marinos, Point of the Seawolves.

51

17-MILE DRIVE

Top left: Pebble Beach is one of the most beautiful private communitites known throughout the world for its natural scenic beauty.

Bottom Left: Cypress Point Golf Course, one of the many beautiful golf courses in this area, is also a site of the annual Crosby Pro-Am Tournament and is ranked among the top in the country.

Above: Twilight view of the Lone Cypress Tree.

Right: Lone Cypress: On the 17-Mile Drive looking south towards Carmel Bay and Point Lobos is the most photographed tree in the world.

MONTEREY PENINSULA AND THE OLD PACIFIC CAPITAL

*"The waves which lap so quietly about the
jetties of Monterey grow louder and larger
in the distance; you can see the breakers
leaping high and white by day; at night, the
outline of the shore is traced in transparent
silver by the moonlight and the flying foam;
and from all round, even in quiet weather,
the low, distant, thrilling roar of the
Pacific hangs over the coast and the adjacent
country like smoke above a battle.*
Robert Louis Stevenson*

A port city and resort on the central coast of California, Monterey is about 125 miles south of San Francisco and is situated on Monterey Bay. It is the largest city on the Monterey Peninsula and is the neighbor of lovely communities named Carmel, Seaside, Del Rey Oaks, Pacific Grove, and Sand City.

It is an exquisite area...beaming with white beaches broken by ragged cliffs and stands of cypress trees and pine. A unique California product of cultural and historical significance, it is a blend of Spanish, New England, missions and ranches...and of sea and sand.

Monterey Peninsula was discovered back in 1542 by Juan Cabrillo, a Portuguese who worked under the Spanish crown. An experienced navigator, Cabrillo explored nearly 800 miles of present-day California shoreline, locating and naming many places and laying claim to all the territory for Spain. Spain had more than a passing interest in the settlement of California. The possibility of finding gold there, was an everpresent hope and the legend of the Straits of Anian (reputedly the shortest Northwest Passage to the wealth of Cathay) continued to be an important goal, particularly since Spain felt it would be an important strategic location in event of foreign control of the mythical straits. No gold was found. And the legendary straits remained elusive.

Cabrillo died and it wasn't until 1602, that another Spanish explorer. Sebastian Vizcaino, sailed into the bay under Spain's reluctant permission. He charted and explored the same places which Cabrillo had traversed, and renamed all the points to suit his fancy. Today San Diego, Monterey, Buena Ventura, Santa Barbara and others are the names Vizcaino chose as he proceeded up the coast back in the early 1600's. Vizcaino named the bay for the Count of Monte-Rey, the Viceroy of Mexico.

Though Vizcaino's expedition was considered a success, Mexico City changed its officials and elected a new viceroy, a man who harbored jealous feeling about his successful predecessor. This new viceroy, Juan de Mendoza y Luna, turned his interests in explorations elsewhere, and possibilities of colonization took a back seat. It would be another 170 or so years before the first settlement would be founded. And it would be through the introduction of a new element...the mission.

Overleaf: The fog adds a great deal of serenity
and peace to this view of Monterey Bay.
Beautiful in both sunshine and fog.

Overleaf: One of California's first villages in the mid-19th century, Monterey has a heritage of Mexican and Spanish cultures that still linger here. Monterey at one time was both the Mexican and Californian capital.

Left: One of the most interesting sights in Monterey is Fisherman's Wharf where so many different and unique activities take place.

Below: Many sailing and pleasure craft line the moorings in Monterey Harbor adjoining Fisherman's Wharf.

The Spanish crown felt that missions would be the only way to save the souls of the natives. Through Christianization and retraining, Spain felt the natives would become useful citizens under Spanish rule. Through missions, it was believed that it would take approximately ten years to convert the Indians. Naturally, to accomplish this task in ten years was an over ambitious goal and most of the missions lasted well over ten years. Many others lasted over a century.

The first mission, San Carlos de Borromeo del Rio Carmelo, was established in 1770 by Father Junipero Serra. Father Serra was described as "an enthusiastic, battling, almost quarrelsome, fearless, keen-witted, fervidly devout, unselfish, single-minded missionary". Perhaps an exaggerated characterization; nevertheless, Father Serra played a very important role in the settlement of this area in California, some 250 years after the first settlement of the Pacific coast.

Because Spanish occupation was late, and because of California's topography which effectively isolated people and made migration difficult, the Spanish domination was very tenuous.

In 1775, the King of Spain reorganized the settlement, and declared Monterey the capital of California. It was to remain the capital until 1849, except for a short time in the 1840's.

Other visitors, the French, the British, the Russians, came to explore this region and all reported that the Spanish presence was very tentative. Strategic ports were unorganized. Settlements were poorly developed. Deficiencies in the Spanish regime was very obvious and there was a strong awareness of Spain's vulnerability. The region continued to attract interest, particularly among Americans who knew its potential. Fishing, furs, and pearls provided new wealth. Of real interest was the California otter which was prized for its pelt and commanded hundreds of dollars, especially in the Orient. Those persons who could trade knives, hatchets, and even mirrors with Indians for these pelts made fortunes. In the early 1800's, American ships on a single voyage, procured thousands upon thousands of pelts. Because of Spain's lack of power, there was little to be done to protect its own interest in the fur trade.

Ultimately, overtrapping occured and the California sea otter was nearly driven to extinction. Thanks to protective measures, the otter has managed to make a comback along the coastal waters of California.

In 1822, the region became part of the Mexican Republic, and Spain's brief tenure came to an end. During this time, California's first constitution was drawn up at a legislative meeting in Monterey. The seeds of opposition to Mexican rule were planted by the Yankee fishermen and traders, and in July of 1846 the United States took possession of Monterey from Mexico. Commodore Sloate, commander of the United States fleet in the Pacific, formally claimed California by raising the American flag over the Custom House, thus bringing 600,000 square miles into the Union.

The discovery of gold was ever elusive. The Spanish, the Mexicans, and the Americans had as yet to find the placer deposits which were to make California so historical. Though there were indications that gold was there, with bits of gold being found by a few panhandlers and Indians, it wasn't until 1848 that a transplanted Yankee named James Wilson Marshall, found THE gold. Marshall was not looking for it. He was at work constructing a sawmill on the American River, and allowing the river to run through the trailrace during the night in order to broaden and deepen it. One morning, after shutting off the water, he stepped into the race, and there...about six inches below the water...he saw gold.

Word got out, much as Marshall tried to keep it secret, and the famous gold rush was on. Over the next few years, thousands of people became professional miners, and many other placer deposits were discovered. Between 1849 and the end of the century, a total of $1,300,000,000 was mined.

Left: U.S. Naval Postgraduate School, was moved to Monterey from Annapolis, Maryland in 1951. It provides advanced education for officers in engineering and professional naval subjects.

Below: U.S. Army Language Center.

After the gold rush of 1849, Monterey declined to such a state, that San Francisco replaced it as the leading metropolis. Monterey became a whaling center and built canneries and fisheries along its harbors. Famous American novelist, John Steinbeck, was inspired to write CANNERY ROW and SWEET THURSDAY when he visited the sardine fisheries among the calm harbor and red-roofed stucco houses. In his famous fictional novel CANNERY ROW, he vividly describes the sardine industry: "Cannery Row in Monterey in California is a poem, a stink, a grating noise, a quality of light, a tone, a habit, a nostalgia, a dream....In the morning when the sardine fleet has made a catch, the purse-seiners waddle heavily into the bay blowing their whistles. The deep-laden boats pull in against the coast where the canneries dip their tails into the bay...Then cannery whistles scream and all over the town men and women scramble into their clothes and come running down to the Row to got to work...They come running to clean and cut and pack and cook and can the fish. The whole street rumbles and growns and screams and rattles while the silver rivers of fish pour in out of the boats and the boats rise higher and higher in the water until they are empty. The canneries rumble and rattle and squeak until the last fish is cleaned and cut and cooked and canned and then the whistles scream again...and Cannery Row becomes itself again—quiet and magical. Its normal life returns."

With the canneries now silent, art galleries, gourmet restaurants and a Fisherman's Wharf have taken over the Row. Every important historic landmark and old house of distinction can be seen by following the "Path of History", an orange-red line painted down the center of the streets throughout the town. The only mission remaining in California in continous use since 1795 called the Royal Presidio Chapel, has the most ornate facade of all California's chapels. There are a number of other famous landmarks along the "Path of History". The Robert Louis Stevenson House, his home for three months during 1879, is preserved as a small state historical monument and contains a large collection of memorabilia. California's First Theatre, originally built as an adobe boarding-house and saloon, is here. And of course, the oldest Mexican custom house, built in 1827, has been preserved to commemorate the raising of our American flag by Commodore Sloat in 1846. The Larkin House, named for Thomas Larkin, the first and only United States consul to Mexico, can be seen; as well as the Casa del Oro (House of Gold), a restored general store which is full of trade items used during Monterey's early history. The old town hall and public school built during the Mexican War is of Classic Revival design, and is the building in which the first constitution of California was written. It is called the Colton Hall Museum. Downstairs is the Old Monterey Jail.

A famous scenic drive, the Seventeen mile Drive between Monterey and Carmel along the Pacific Coast, takes a driver past Seal Rock, Cypress Point, and Spyglass Hill and Pebble Beach golf courses. In late January, the Bing Crosby Pro-Amateur Golf Championship is held here.

Monterey is also the site of the U.S. Naval Postgraduate School, the Defense Language Institute, Monterey Peninsula College and Monterey Institute of Foreign Studies. One of the largest army installations in the country, Fort Ord, is nearby.

Top left: Cannery Row Square: "The Row" prospers today. Further down Cannery Row, in addition to the local "characters" who still live here and call "The Row" home, many interesting shops and boutiques filled with unique items as well as antique shops and art galleries dot "The Row" providing the visitors hours of shopping and "browsing".

Bottom left: Point Joe and The Restless Sea, many ships have been shipwrecked on these rocks when their masters have mistaken this point for the entrance to Monterey Bay. While the sea in this view is calm, it can become very turbulent.

Left and below: These playful Harbor Seals, can be found in and around Monterey Bay. They are loved by natives and tourists alike.

Overleaf: Magic Carpet at Pacific Grove.

JOURNEY OF
THE MONARCHS

Please, lovely monarch, explain your migration.
Why do you fly to this coastal location?
Is it the surf and the nice sunny weather,
Or is it the nectar and water you savor?

Tell us, little one, so silent and sweet —
Is it because you have friends to meet?
Have you a special, mystical mission?
How do you travel . . . by some intuition?

Each year, Pacific Grove residents watch in amazement at the sight. Butterflies. . .tens of thousands of monarch butterflies! They cling motionless, with folded wings, to every branch and trunk of eucalyptus trees. They swirl like masses of Fall leaves in the wind, and carpet the ground in orange-golden multitude. It is October. The monarchs have arrived on schedule.

This yearly migration of monarchs to winter havens in Florida, Texas, Mexico, and California has baffled scientist for decades. Their migration is a marvelous, intricate pattern of behaviour for which only a few of its aspects is understood.

Just about every romping youngster and meadow walker knows this colorful butterfly by sight and probably by name. It darts, dips and flutters in summer over pastures, fields, and yards all over the United States and Southern Canada. In winter, it leaves the colder climates, flying hundreds of miles to certain destinations with uncanning accuracy.

The western monarch population, DANAUS PLEXIPPUS, migrates to several winter havens along the California coast. Their Pacific Grove wintering ground is the most famous, attracting yearly visitors to the "butterfly trees". Eucalyptus trees simply pulsate with what appears to be thousands of tiny stained glass windows, branches bending low and sometimes breaking under the weight. One hundred monarchs clustered together barely weigh one ounce, and branches as wide as three inches have snapped under the burden of these languid butterflies!

Monarchs have long been known to fly great distances and to migrate, like birds, according to seasonal changes and reproductive cycles. There is little doubt that their southward migration is simply a way to escape winter's killing frost. Because the entire lifespan of a monarch is no more than nine or ten months, these butterflies desert their breeding grounds, fly south, and then return north only once before they die. The great intrigue is that in each succeeding generation, the migratory pattern is repeated, as though a blueprint had been passed along from parent to child.

The typical lifespan of a monarch wintering in Pacific Grove goes something like this: As a young adult, it arrives sometime in October, not in flocks, but more or less singly. There it settles among thousands of friends on a tree, in an almost comatose state. In the coolness of the evening air, it closes its wings, showing the lighter color of its underwings and looking very much like a dead leaf. When the sun comes up and the air is warmed, it stretches its wings, unfolding to show the brilliant orange wing surface with which we are all so familiar. Once the monarch is revitalized by the warmth of the sun, it rouses and flutters off to feed on an exclusive diet of nectar and water. The monarch will winter over in Pacific Grove until sometime in March. It will have mated and now it will begin its long northward journey home.

It may travel 1,000 miles or more, through wind and rain, across plains and over mountains, at a cruising speed of 10 miles an hour. On the way, each female will lay hundreds of eggs, one at a time, on young milkweed plants. The larvae feeds only on a certain genus of milkweed, a characteristic which has given the monarch another name...the milkweed butterfly.

It is interesting to note that certain species of milkweed produce a poisonous substance which can be accumulated by the larvae and then carried over into the adult monarch during metamorphoses. Should the monarch become a birds' meal, the poison causes the bird to vomit, and the bird learns to refrain from eating orange and black butterflies. Certainly a curious protective measure which helps to maintain the monarch population growth.

Some females, not yet ready to lay eggs, may journey on to the final destination. It takes about five weeks for larvae to transform into adult butterflies, so all along the journey home, where eggs have been deposited, fresh new monarchs are born.

Most of the male monarchs die on the journey northward, and a great percentage of now scruffy, tired and bedraggled females die too. Those monarchs who reach adulthood toward the end of summer make the migration south to Pacific Grove. The whole proceedure is repeated with this new generation of butterflies.

An astonishing and recent suggestion about the monarch's breeding cycle is that two separate kinds of monarchs are hatched...migratory and non-migratory. A non-migratory butterfly undergoes transformation or metamorphoses in the early summer on the journey north, and only survives for approximately one month. It is these non-migrating monarchs who, toward the end of summer, lay the traveling generation which can live close to ten months.

For years, lepidopterists have been marking these butterflies in hope of learning more about their migrations and guidance systems. Zoologists have known that at least two distinct populations exist in North America...one in the eastern part of the country and the other in the midwest and the west. Since numerous wintering sites for the western monarch population were known to exist along the California coast, lepidopterists suspected a similar site had to exist for the eastern population.

Tagging or marking these frail insects had been a dismal failure until 1952, when a Canadian zoologist named Fred A. Urquhart, developed a way to band a wing with the same kind of pressure sensitive label used to price glassware. He printed thousands of labels with numbers and his return address, and then began an appeal for volunteers who would net and tag monarchs. Over the years, thousands of monarchs have been tagged all across the continent and records of date, time, place, sex and numbers have been mailed to Urquhart. As the information came in, Urquhart would map out, with small dots, the movement of captured and recaptured monarchs, and eventually had a line of dots which converged in Mexico. With the aid of a volunteer who was working in Mexico City, the wintering site for the eastern monarch population was finally discovered in January of 1975. In a forest northwest of Mexico City, a 20-acre enclave was brimming with millions of monarchs, a thrilling climax to Urquhart's diligent and long study. Thousands of these monarchs were tagged to begin plotting their path back home.

Monarch Butterflies from all over the western Unites States migrate here from October through March.

Just why monarchs have chosen certain roosting areas is still not answered, but one interesting hypothesis is that the monarch butterfly evolved in Mexico thousands of years ago and Mexico is actually its home. As glaciers receded and the climates warmed, the monarch extended its breeding grounds farther northward in the summer, and now returns ''home'' in the winter months. Over the eras, the distance to home grew greater, and nature adjusted the monarch's programming to include a progeny which today, mysteriously can return to its original home.

A tempting hypothesis it is. Meanwhile, Pacific Grove residents are grateful simply for having this puzzling but beautiful enigma occur yearly at their door. Justifiably they have named their community ''Butterfly Town, U.S.A.'', and fiercely protect the migration grounds of this remarkable and elusive butterfly…the monarch.

Overleaf: Reflective moods of the
ocean and sun capture this
beautiful sunset at Carmel Beach.

Above: The Golden Poppy is
California's State Flower.